J
797.3
Hol
Holden
Wind and surf

602574
12.95

DATE DUE			

ALL ACTION

WIND AND
SURF

PHIL HOLDEN

LERNER PUBLICATIONS COMPANY
MINNEAPOLIS

Titles in this series

Backpacking
Canoeing
Climbing
Mountain Biking
Skiing
Skateboarding
Survival Skills
Wind and Surf

All photographs by Phil Holden, except 32, 33 (both Oxford Scientific Films) and 34 (Bob Allen).

Front cover: A windsurfer executes an acrobatic leap.

First published in the United States in 1992
by Lerner Publications Company

Copyright © 1991 Wayland (Publishers) Limited
First published in 1991 by Wayland (Publishers) Ltd.
612 Western Rd, Hove, East Sussex BN3 1JD England

Library of Congress Cataloging-in-Publication Data
Holden, Phil.
   Wind and surf / Phil Holden.
      p.   cm. — (All action)
   Includes index.
   Summary: Examines the history and techniques of surfing and windsurfing and discusses safety precautions and some top surfers and windsurfers.
   ISBN 0-8225-2477-5
   1. Surfing—Juvenile literature.   2. Windsurfing—Juvenile literature.   [1. Surfing. 2. Windsurfing.]   I. Title.
II. Series.
GV840.S8H65 1991
797.3'2—dc20   91-17862
                                                          CIP
                                                          AC

Printed in Italy
Bound in the United States of America
1 2 3 4 5 6 7 8 9 10 00 99 98 97 96 95 94 93 92 91

Contents

INTRODUCTION

A lthough it seems like a new sport, surfing is as old as the Polynesian islands of the central Pacific. For centuries the islanders have ridden the surf over the coral reefs that surround the islands. They have always had to live in harmony with the ocean to survive. It is where they get most of their food. When the Polynesians could not fish because of rough weather, they surfed for fun. They swam out to the breaking waves, turned, and surfed back to the beach on their chests. Nowadays this is called **bodysurfing**.

If you are a good swimmer, you may have gone to the ocean and done exactly what the Polynesians first did hundreds of years ago. If you enjoyed it, use this book to find out how to have even more fun in the sea. You can use a foam **bodyboard**, a surfboard, or a windsurfer. There are surf spots on the coasts of many countries in the world. You can go windsurfing, or boardsailing, on any large lake, as well as on the ocean.

The biggest waves anywhere are those off the north shore of the Hawaiian island Oahu. When Captain

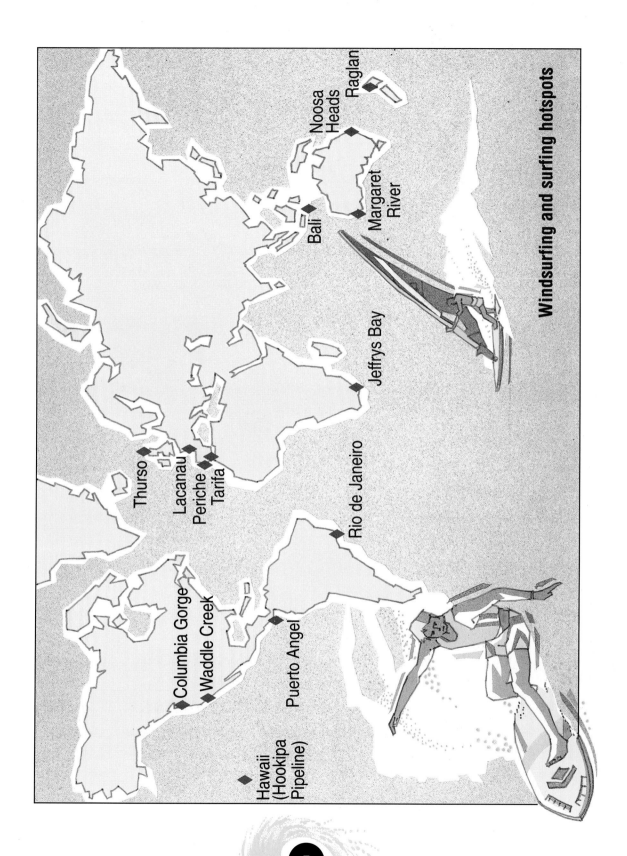

Windsurfing and surfing hotspots

Raglan
Noosa Heads
Margaret River
Bali
Jeffrys Bay
Thurso
Lacanau
Periche
Tarifa
Rio de Janeiro
Columbia Gorge
Waddle Creek
Puerto Angel
Hawaii (Hookipa Pipeline)

James Cook, the famous explorer, arrived in 1778, surfing competitions were regularly held. There were even a few professional surfers! In 1907, Jack London, who wrote the adventure book *The Call of the Wild*, returned to California from Hawaii with a design for a surfboard. It was based on the solid wood boards he had seen on Oahu. It was so heavy that at least three people were needed to carry it to the beach, and it was about twice as long as London was tall! The sport quickly caught on in Australia and California, where crowds of spectators were inspired by **malibu surfers** such as Duke Kahanamoku.

With modern materials, the boards of today are amazingly strong and light. It is now possible to swim in very cold water because wetsuits can keep you warm. The wetsuit is the second most important piece of **gear** in countries with cold water, such as Great Britain, New Zealand, Canada, and many parts of the United States.

It was the development of the wetsuit that led to the spread of surfing all around the world during the 1950s and 1960s.

Since then, the sport has developed into three main areas — bodyboarding, malibu surfing, and windsurfing. Bodyboarding and malibu surfing are basically the same thing, except that one is done while lying down on a board and the other is done standing up. Windsurfing is quite a bit different.

In the early 1950s, Peter Chilvers of the United Kingdom (Great Britian and Northern Ireland) attached a sail to a surfboard to move it around. At roughly the same time, Hoyle Schweitzer of the United States began to make windsurfers similar to

ABOVE

Surfing has always drawn crowds of admiring spectators.

RIGHT

Michelle Donoghue, one of the world's top surfers.

those you can see out on the water now. So who invented the windsurfer? No one really knows — Chilvers and Schweitzer are still arguing about it! In any case, by the mid-1960s windsurfers made it possible to ride waves without having to paddle out to them. The sport grew quickly among surfers, as well as among sailors who liked the fact that they could sometimes go twice as fast on a windsurfer as they could in a sailboat.

B oth windsurfers and surfers are great adventurers. The search for the best waves and wind has taken them to uninhabited islands in the Pacific, shark-infested waters off the coast of Africa, and very cold seas off the Pacific coasts of Canada and the United States. There is no

ABOVE

Two windsurfers explore a hidden beach.

feeling in the world that matches the one you get flying across the surface of the ocean, powered only by the waves or the wind.

Years ago, the sight of another surfer or windsurfer heading to the beach was a fairly rare thing. If you saw one you would certainly wave, and probably stop and talk. People are still very friendly, but if you stopped and spoke to everyone you met on the way to the beach these days, you would never get there! This book explains why surfing and windsurfing have become so popular and how you can get involved.

FIRST STEPS

You need to be able to swim well before you go out on the ocean. Swimming at least four lengths of an average pool without a break will give you some idea of what it could be like to be separated from your board and have to swim to the shore. Of course, as well as having to swim a long way, you will have to fight the waves and currents.

Unless you are confident swimming over such distances, it would be very dangerous for you to go surfing or windsurfing on the ocean.

The best and safest way to start is with a group of friends who want to learn surfing or windsurfing too. Many coastal or lakeside towns have surfing or windsurfing clubs that give lessons and rent equipment. Maybe your school does too. You will learn much more quickly if you can watch the mistakes other people make and get others to tell you where you are going wrong. At the start it is a good idea to split the cost of gear with a friend — neither of you can surf all day, so take turns. Even bodyboards can cost a lot of money, and you could buy a good used car for the cost of some windsurfers!

Wetsuits are used in places where the water is too cold to swim in only a swimsuit. Wetsuits come in many shapes and sizes — long legs and arms (full), short legs and arms

ABOVE

You will need a wetsuit for surfing, especially if the conditions are as cold as this!

LEFT

These people have chosen to learn to surf at a surf school in France.

(shortie) and combinations of the two. They come in thicknesses ranging from 2.5 millimeters (mm) to 5mm and in many different colors. The information box on page 19 will give you some idea of what kind you might need.

Even if the water is very warm, you should wear some sort of wetsuit, in case you get into trouble and have to spend hours in the water. Even a wetsuit vest can keep you from getting hypothermia, in which your body temperature falls below normal.

The easiest sort of surfing to learn is bodyboarding. The boards are made of lightweight foam and are about a yard long. They are not very expensive, so they are a good choice for beginners. Although the basic technique of bodyboarding is very easy, the experts do things like jumps and spins on the wave, maneuvers which take years of practice.

Surfing and windsurfing can be very hard work. Bodyboarding is easier, but no less exciting. It is a very close relation of the bodysurfing that the Polynesian islanders have done for centuries.

Bodyboarders wear **flippers** on their feet to help them travel more quickly through the waves. The whole experience can be much less tiring with flippers.

A natural progression from bodyboarding is kneeboarding, which uses a faster and harder board. Catch the wave while lying down as you would in bodyboarding, but ride from a kneeling position. Kneeboarding is quite unusual — you are more likely to see a bodyboarder kneeling on her or his bodyboard than on a real kneeboard.

BELOW

Bodyboarding is a good introduction to surfing, because it is easy to learn and the equipment is inexpensive.

Personalities in Surfing

Wendy Botha (above)

Wendy Botha first started surfing at age 14 at Hearn Beach, South Africa. Having won most of the titles in South Africa, she emigrated to Australia. At 25, she was the reigning world champion. She first won the championships in 1986.

Martin Potter

Martin Potter is originally from England but has lived most of his life in South Africa. After 13 years surfing, he developed a radical surfing style based on aerials and wild cutbacks. Consistency gave him first place in the 1990 tour.

Surfing greats

Duke Kahanamoku: *The world's first famous surfer.*
Gerry Lopez: *Changed the style of surfing from a laid-back gliding approach to radical, fast moves.*
Mark Richards: *Popularized the twin fin board and flying bottom turns.*
Martin Potter: *The 1990 world tour champion; the first ever born in the United Kingdom*

Malibu surfing is the most popular kind of surfing. A long, stiff **fiberglass** board is used. As a rough guide, the board you learn on should be about 1-1/2 feet (about 50 centimeters) taller than you are. As you get better, you can use smaller boards. Big boards catch waves more easily, but they turn slowly.

To catch a wave, move your board toward it by paddling with your arms. Once you have caught a wave, stand up quickly with your feet across the board. Then you can control your path along the wave by tilting the board to one side or the other. A surfing instructor will tell you about basic safety, your choice of gear, and where to position yourself on the beach for the right wave. You will also find out about paddling, **duck diving**, standing up - or "taking off" — and riding along the face of the wave. With two or three days of the right conditions — a small wave of less than one yard (or one meter) is ideal for learning — most people can master the basics.

Windsurfing takes malibu surfing a step further, by adding a sail to power the board. It is easiest to learn how to maneuver the board on flat water in light winds, using a large board that is **buoyant** and stable. After you learn how to handle the board, you can try in rougher water. The basic techniques for windsurfing are rigging (putting the sail, mast, and boom together), uphauling (lifting the **rig** out of the water), **tacking**

RIGHT

Windsurfing uses the power of the wind to move the board, as well as the power of the waves.

(turning into the wind), and **jibing** (turning downwind).

Learning the basics of windsurfing usually does not take as long as learning the basics of surfing. If you go in the right conditions it might only take you a day before you can sail around happily. Once you have mastered basic windsurfing, there are a number of paths that you can take. Wave sailing combines the forces of wind and surf. It is the most difficult of the disciplines to master and takes place in strong cross-shore winds (which come toward the shore at an angle) and large waves. Wave sailing offers the chance to soar high into the air, doing turns and **freestyle** tricks. Because of this, it is also the most dangerous.

Course windsurfing is most popular among people who are used to sailing in boats, where competition involves racing around a fixed course. It involves sailing over long distances and is possible even in light winds. The boards used for course racing are much longer and more buoyant than wave boards and are also suitable for freestyle tricks.

Slalom combines wave sailing with course racing. Using a board longer

BELOW

On flat water, windsurfers are capable of going extremely fast, as in this slalom race.

than a wave board but shorter than a racing board, slalom competitors race around a short course as quickly as possible. The slalom course is designed for speed, with no slow upwind legs. Because the boards all go at roughly the same speed, races are won and lost at the turns.

The final windsurfing discipline is speed sailing. The only aim is to go fast — so fast that many of the competitors wear a crash helmet! The boards are specially built and are incredibly narrow. Sail designers use computers and aerodynamic test tunnels. The record for the fastest

ABOVE

In speed trials, windsurfers go so quickly that the riders have to wear crash helmets!

windsurfer is over 44 **knots** per hour (about 50 miles or 81 kilometers per hour).

The number and variety of boards you can buy in most surf shops seems terrifying at first glance. You should go to a dealership that specializes in windsurfing equipment for your first board. The sales staff will be able to help you find exactly what you need. Shop around

Arnaud and Jenna de Rosnay

Arnaud and Jenna seemed to be the perfect windsurfing couple. He was a member of the French aristocracy given to eccentric adventures. She was a glamorous model and mother. Then the bubble burst. On November 24, 1984, while trying to cross the Taiwan Strait between Taiwan and China on a windsurfer, Arnaud disappeared. He has never been seen since.

The best type of board to learn on is one that is very buoyant and has a small sail attached to it.

Board fashion through time

Bonzer: *Tail channels, a large central fin and two smaller rail fins.*
Quad fin: *Four equal-sized fins on a fat-tailed board.*
Thruster: *All-around board with three equal-sized fins; still very popular.*
Twin fin: *Short board with wide square tail and two fins.*
Single fin pintail: *Narrow tail with one large fin. Still popular in big surf.*

at various windsurfing stores for the best price. Ask other windsurfers which stores they like best. In any case, most new boards will do the job the maker says they will. The main consideration is usually how much the board will cost. Cheaper boards are tougher than more expensive ones, so your first board can cost very little. Later, you can move up to a lighter and faster board.

One way of getting a cheap first board is to buy second-hand. Be very careful! You may never be able to find the person you bought it from

again, so you have to be sure that there is nothing wrong with it. The only way to do this is to take along a friend who knows what to look for. If you do this, you stand a good chance of picking up a board very cheaply indeed.

After cost, another important consideration is the **volume** of the board. A board that is too buoyant (has a lot of volume) will skip over the water and be hard to turn. One that lies too low in the water (and has too little volume) will make balancing and catching waves more difficult. To start with, choose a board with a rounded, wide design that makes it stable and easy to control. Narrow boards are very difficult to turn and hard to stand up on because they will tip over easily.

Once you get your equipment, you will have to learn how to maintain it. Bodyboards do not need much maintenance because they are made almost entirely out of foam. Aside from the board, the only other gear you need is a wetsuit, some flippers

BELOW

A cutaway sail, one of windsurfing's short-lived fads.

Surfers and windsurfers both use grip tape to keep their feet on the board.

for your feet, and a **leash** so that you do not lose your board in a **wipeout.**

The outer fiberglass casing of modern windsurfers and surfboards can crack or shatter as a result of a collision or a wipeout in big waves. If water gets into a crack, further weakening of the board may occur. It is a good idea to seal any **dings** before putting the board back in the water. Use a fiberglass repair kit, which you can buy from most surf shops. It is possible to fix the board temporarily by covering dings with packing tape. This may also keep water from getting in and prevent any accidental cuts you might get from loose fiberglass strands. But it will not work for long, so make sure you repair the damage as soon as possible.

Surfboards need a layer of wax

on the deck to allow you to grip the deck with your feet. More and more people have begun using deck grip — self-adhesive non-slip patches.

Wetsuits come in all shapes, sizes and colors. In some, the panels are glued and "blind-stitched," meaning the **neoprene** is sewn through on one side only. On the other side, it is glued and lined to provide strength and insulation. This is the warmest sort of wetsuit. Make sure that you have tried on a wetsuit before you buy one. It must fit tightly over your stomach and the middle of your back but have enough flexibility in the legs and shoulders. Jump up and down, stretch your arms as high as you can, and pretend to swim. Does the wetsuit rub anywhere? Is it too tight? Is there too much room in it? Bear in mind that wetsuits will stretch slightly when they get wet, so it is good to buy one that seems a bit tight.

Windsurfers choose different sails for different conditions. Sail sizes vary from about 2 to 10 square meters. The size you use depends on how windy it is, how heavy you are, and how good you are. When you buy gear, make sure that it will fit the equipment you already have. This is especially true if it is second-hand and there is no one to ask, aside from the person selling it to you. It is a horrible feeling to get home and find out that the mast you have just bought is too short for the sail for which you bought it.

It also pays to be sure of what you want before you go and buy it. Make sure you visit a reputable windsurfing store, where you know the sales-people will give you good advice.

Your gear will last a lot longer if you rinse out the salt and sand with fresh water after you have been out on saltwater. This is especially important for your wetsuit.

Wetsuits

Long john: *The original wetsuit. Only really suitable for warm water. Warmer if combined with a wetsuit jacket.*
Shortie: *One-piece with short arms and legs. Suitable for warm water only.*
Convertible: *A shortie to which you can strap full length arms and legs. Cool water.*
Steamer: *Full-body one-piece. Cold water.*

THE OCEAN

It is a good idea to be able to predict what the weather might be like for surfing or windsurfing from a TV weather forecast. (TV weather forecasters rarely seem to say anything like, "A low-pressure system in the Atlantic means that conditions will be ideal for surfing tomorrow"!) To predict when the best waves and wind will appear, you need to know how they are formed.

Strong winds usually come with areas of low pressure. The air in these systems moves around the center. This kind of weather system occurs most often in the winter, causing sudden changes in wind strength and direction. Luckily, weather maps and meteorological reports are constantly updated and this data is available from television, radio, and newspaper weather reports. Valley basins, cliffs, and the nature of the surrounding coastline may also increase the wind strength.

At Sotovento in Fuerteventura, one of the Canary Islands, the warmth from the sun can accelerate the wind

LEFT

High winds such as these are very dangerous. Only experts should attempt to sail in them.

to speeds regularly exceeding 37 mph (about 60 kph). As the land warms up in the afternoon, the air above it warms and rises. Cold air from over the sea rushes in to replace the warm air.

Waves are made when storms out in the middle of the ocean form **swells**. These swells arrive on exposed beaches two or three days after their formation in mid-ocean, having traveled hundreds of miles. If the local winds are offshore (blowing from the shore toward the sea), conditions are set for a perfect day's surfing. If they are cross-shore, the weather is right for windsurfing. The best waves are found at beaches on coasts that face the ocean swells.

Sand banks and shallow areas lying at an angle to the approaching swells cause the waves to **peel** (break away in sequence) along the beach. Without a good bank, the waves will **close out** (break at the same time all along their length).

ABOVE

Going out on the ocean can be a dangerous experience, especially in conditions like these.

Whether the **tide** is in or out also affects the sort of waves that hit the beach. Waves break when they reach water that is slightly deeper than they are high. If a beach slopes gently at low tide but gets deep very suddenly at high tide, low tide will be a good time to surf. This is because at high tide the waves reach the depth at which they break at almost the same time as they hit the beach – you will not have long to surf the wave before you hit the beach too! Get to know what height of tide produces the best waves at your regular spot and use tide tables to plan your trips. Otherwise you could spend hours waiting on the beach for a good wave.

BELOW

Always be aware
of where other
sailors are, so
that you don't run
.them over and
injure them.

Tidal bores exist in places such as where river currents meet ocean tides. These are caused by the funneling effect of the coastline and very high tides of about 14 yards (about 13m) and higher. This sort of river wave can be ridden for distances of up to three miles (about 5k) at a time!

People such as Gerry Lopez and Robbie Naish have earned their worldwide glory at Hawaii. Because the islands are in deep water, the waves that reach them travel with almost no loss of size. They are also in the center of the Pacific, and exposed to swells formed almost anywhere in the ocean. Off the west coasts of Great Britain, Spain, Portugal, and France, deep water causes other huge waves, but they are less common.

HOW IT'S DONE

Standing with a bodyboard in shallow surf and launching yourself onto the board as the wave passes is a good way to start. You will find catching waves much easier if you are already traveling almost as fast as the wave and in the same direction. So push off as hard as you can just before the wave reaches you.

The speed and power you feel as you are picked up by a wave is much greater if you can get farther from shore, where the waves first begin to break. To do this you will need a pair of flippers. It is best to put these on at the water's edge, so that you do not fall over trying to walk down the shore in them. To keep your gear from getting lost during a wipeout, use retainers that attach the flippers to your ankles and a leash that attaches the board to your wrist.

Move along by kicking your legs up and down while lying down on the board. Keep your weight as far forward as possible. By doing this, you can swim more easily to where the waves break, and you can catch the waves more smoothly when you get there. Carefully choose the waves you catch — those that break slowly and

ABOVE and BELOW

Learn to bodyboard by standing in shallow water and pushing off as the waves go past.

ABOVE

Once you have
mastered the
basic technique
you will be able to
paddle out to
where the waves
break and are
more powerful.

continuously along their length will
be the most enjoyable to ride. The
best place to hop onto a wave is a
few yards down from where it breaks.

As the wave comes toward you,
turn toward the shore and accelerate
down the front of the wave. If the

wave is peeling quickly, point yourself
slightly away from it. Before your speed
drops, lean your weight in toward the
wave so that you are surfing along it
instead of away from it. Getting into
the **critical section** and staying there
is what it's all about. This is the part of

the wave where there is the most power, speed, and excitement.

If you are learning to surf, practice paddling in shallow water, with your weight forward on the board. Try to paddle with the nose of the board just clear of the water. Use alternate strokes, like the ones you use when swimming the front crawl, to get through the waves to the spot where you want to catch a wave. Use your body weight to sink the nose of the board under the waves that come toward you while you are paddling out. This will keep them from pushing you back too far. It is called duck diving.

Use powerful strokes when trying to catch a wave, so that you are going at the same speed, and in the same direction, as it is. Once the wave is carrying you along, push down with your arms and swing your legs in underneath you to land square on the board. You can practice this movement on the ground – draw an outline of your board so that you can tell if you are landing with your feet in the right place. The movement brings you to your feet and moves your weight forward, which accelerates the board before you make the turn along the wave. This stage can be very frustrating because it seems as if you will never stand up properly.

When you finally do manage to stand up on a board for the first time, you will be thrilled.

If your right leg falls naturally at the back of the board, you are a "natural foot." Waves breaking from right to left (as you look from the shore), will be easier for you to ride, because you will be able to see the wave better. If your left leg falls at the back of the board you are a "goofy foot." Waves breaking in the opposite direction will be easiest to ride.

S tart learning to windsurf with a flat, stable board in light wind. It is easiest to learn with a group of friends. Until you get used to handling the rig (mast, boom, and sail), use a small sail that will not pull you over even in a gust. About 4 meters square is a good size to learn with.

At the water's edge, unfurl the sail and put the mast and **battens** into their sleeves. Do not tighten the battens yet. Attach the boom to the mast at a height just below your

BELOW

Taking off. Paddle hard, and as the wave starts to carry you along, push down with your hands as you stand up.

Uphauling. Use your knees rather than bending your back, and slide the rig out of the water.

shoulders. Remove horizontal creases in the sail by tightening the **downhaul**. Remove vertical creases with the **outhaul** and the battens. Insert the mast into the mast track.

To begin sailing, pull the rig out of the water by sliding it out sideways. Bend your knees instead of your back while pulling so that you won't injure yourself. Once there is only a corner of the sail in the water, move the hand that will be at the back of the boom to the top of the **uphaul**. Cross your other hand over it to the top of the boom. When you are balanced, grab the boom with your other hand

as well and pull the rig toward you. Once you start moving, the board will move downwind if you lean the rig forward and upwind if you lean it backward.

Windsurfers turn around in two ways. When turning upwind you tack and when turning downwind you jibe. The easiest way for beginners to tack is to move their hands toward the uphaul and get hold of it, dip the tip of the sail in the water and then swing it over the back of the board, while walking around the front.

Once you have mastered that, try doing the same thing without the tip of the sail in the water. Gradually your speed will get better. Eventually, you will be able to tack in seconds, without letting go of the boom until it is time to grab the other side of it.

Jibing should be practiced in the same way at first — by dragging the tip of the sail over the front of the board rather than the back. Because the sail is flipped around by the wind, jibing is usually quicker than tacking, but it is harder.

It is a good idea to use a harness when windsurfing to provide buoyancy, in case of an accident, as well as keeping your arms and shoulders from tiring over long distances. It does so because once you have hooked your harness into the lines on the boom, you can use your body weight instead of your arms to hold the sail.

You must practice self-rescue by derigging the sail on the water and rolling it around the mast. In case the wind drops or you get caught in a storm, you need to paddle the rig and board to the shore, surfer style. This may seem unlikely, but you will have to save yourself at some point, and head-high surf and a storm-force wind is not a good place to learn.

BELOW

You must be able to rescue yourself.

SAFETY

To either side of the shallow white water areas of a surfing break lie deeper channels, where the water brought into the beach by the waves moves back out to sea. This movement of water is known as a rip current. Very experienced surfers occasionally use rip currents to move out to sea, but beginners should stay well clear of them. It is possible to be pulled under by a rip current and drowned, and it happens every year. If you do get caught in a rip current, move along the shore to the nearest area of breaking waves, rather than trying to compete against the current heading out to sea.

Many accidents are caused by people who do not follow surfing rules in crowded conditions. The person nearest the curl has priority and should be left to the wave. Always keep an eye out for other people's safety if they are having trouble. And never steal someone else's wave; other surfers may react violently. Also, you would not want anyone to take one of your waves.

Never surf if you have just eaten a large meal, or you will get cramps.

Never go out in
cold weather
conditions like
these without a
really warm
wetsuit.

LEFT

When the ocean
is this crowded it
is easy for
accidents to
happen. Watch
out!

Make sure you are wearing a warm wetsuit — hypothermia kills people on the sea every year.

Strong offshore winds and outgoing tides are the most dangerous conditions for both surfers and windsurfers, whose boards can be swept out to sea. The best motto for surfers and windsurfers to follow is, "If in doubt, stay out."

SURF DANGERS

In many parts of the world there is a danger of being attacked by a shark. It is hard to guard against shark attack if you live in an area where sharks are active and come close to the shore. A few years ago, some surfers tried painting the bottom of their boards in black and white stripes, because sea snakes are these colors and they are the only animals sharks do not eat. Unfortunately, those boards were no safer than any others. The two main things to remember about sharks are: they feed at night more than in daytime, and they are likely to drift toward the beach on a rising tide. So surfing at dusk while the tide is coming in is a pretty bad idea.

Sea snakes, poisonous jellyfish, and poisonous coral are mostly found in the warm waters of places such as Bali and Hawaii. Consult local surfers or windsurfers to find out if the beach you want to use is dangerous. The Portuguese man-of-war is sometimes found in the waters of northern Europe. These jellyfishlike creatures are blue in color. The tentacles can be up to 11 yards long and cause a nasty sting.

Sea urchins are found on rocky

LEFT

A great white shark. The species is known to have killed several people over the years.

Don't dangle your feet!

Sharks are the ultimate killing and eating machines. Most sharks are unlikely to attack unless they bang into you by accident. They tend to investigate things by biting them to see what happens. Some sharks, including the great white shark that inspired the film Jaws, *attack humans. White sharks, common in the seas of Australia and New Zealand, have been responsible for many deaths.*

ABOVE

Sea urchins like this are common around the coasts of many countries, and can cause a nasty swelling if stepped on.

coastlines all around Europe, and on the Atlantic Ocean and Mediterranean sea shores. These spiny creatures lurk in crevices and holes and pose one of the most common threats to surfers and windsurfers at places like Fuerteventura in the Canary Islands, northwest of Africa, particularly at low tide. Avoid walking over rocks in shallow water whenever you can. Carry a pair of tweezers to remove the spines. Even a small part of the animal left in your foot causes it to swell up.

FITNESS

The best exercise for surfing or windsurfing is the sport itself. But if there is no wind or waves, swimming is a good substitute that will keep you extremely fit. Practice the front crawl over long distances — the muscles you use for this are the same ones as you use when paddling out or sailing. Practice swimming underwater as well — the ability to hold your breath is important in case a wave holds you under the surface for a long time.

There are various exercises that can be done at home or in a gym. The simple push-up is probably the best.

Windsurfing hot spots

Hookipa, on the island of Maui in the central Pacific, is a wave sailing paradise.
Tarifa in Southern Spain is famous for constant wind.
Waddle Creek, San Francisco, is known for powerful waves, good wind, and cold water!
Columbia Gorge, Washington State. If the wind carries you away from your start point, the river carries you back!
Margaret River, New South Wales, Australia, is famous for huge surf.

ABOVE

If you want to compete in top-class events such as the one shown here, you will need to be in good shape.

FAR LEFT

Mountain biking is a very good way to keep in shape for surfing and windsurfing.

Twenty push-ups is a good number to start with – add a few more each week as you progress. Shoulder swings are useful for stretching your muscles, as well as for warming up before you actually go surfing.

Injuries to the knees and back are common among surfers and windsurfers. Bicycling is a good way to strengthen leg and knee muscles. To strengthen your back, lie face up on the ground with your hands behind your head. Then lift your head up slowly, until the base of your back is flat against the ground. Twenty of these will keep you in good shape.

Lacanau Océan Pro

The standard of surfing was raised considerably by the formation of a World Professionals Circuit in 1976. The Association of Surfing Professionals (ASP) is responsible for organizing events throughout the world. The chance to watch or even compete against the world's top professionals has helped many young surfers progress rapidly.

Maneuvers such as **tube** riding, 360 turns, and **floaters** quickly became commonplace once people had seen them performed on the tour. The professionals continually try to push the boundaries of speed and control to stay ahead of the crowd.

During the 1980s, Tom Curren from Santa Barbara, California, set the standards in men's professional surfing. Having won the World Amateurs Junior Division at only 16 years old in France in 1980, he went on to win the World Professionals Open Division in 1985 and again in 1986. Curren had been off the circuit in 1989, but thousands of people flocked to Lacanau, France, in the summer of 1990 to see if Tom still had what it takes to win. This competition is a perfect example of how the top pros go head-to-head.

LEFT

The beach at
Lacanau,
France.

BELOW

Crowds gather
around the
spectator stand
to see who will
win the Océan
Pro.

Each ride in a contest is scored from 1 to 10 according to the surfer's wave choice, the length of the ride, and the number of quality maneuvers that are made in the critical sections. A panel of five judges assesses a maximum of 10 rides for each surfer in a 30-minute heat. The best four rides count. The highest and lowest scores for each judge are discounted, leaving a maximum of 120 points per heat.

Because Curren had been away from the tour for the previous season, he did not get an automatic entry into round three, as other professionals usually get. This meant he had to surf his way through two extra rounds. With a prize of $10,000 available to the winner, the pressure was on from the start in his first heat against a young Australian, Luke Egan. It was a close contest, which Curren won by only two-tenths of a point.

In his next heat against big-wave veteran Gary Elkerton, Curren's determination and contest strategy was beginning to show. Both in this heat and the quarterfinals, Curren took off on a wave as soon as the horn sounded for the start, having carefully positioned himself beforehand.

against fellow American Kelly Slater. Because he is slimmer and lighter, the small surf suited Kelly, who was performing some sharp turns off the lip of the wave, as well as some long forehand **floaters.** To do these, Kelly was waiting until the wave had almost folded in front of him. Then he powered up and over the curl of the wave to float the board over the white water to the next section. The crowd was left wondering how Tom would respond.

Almost immediately, he took off on a large wave. It was a left-hander and, because he is a natural foot, this meant Curren's back was to the wave. He launched his board vertically into the approaching section for a spectacular **re-entry** on the biggest wave of the heat. This wave took him well down the beach, and there the cross-shore drift put him in a great position to choose his final wave. This he rode right to the beach, darting in and out from under the tube and finishing with a switch-foot (changing his left foot to the back of the board) right in front of the spectators at the shoreline.

With this great ride, Tom made it to the final round against yet another

This careful positioning gave him priority over his opponent if both surfers wanted the wave. Curren took four good waves early on and shielded his opponent from others that were as good. He then waited, picking off the bigger and faster waves to make up his maximum of 10.

The semifinals saw Curren up

The American
Ritchie Collins
(above) launches
a floater as part of
his bid to defeat
the eventual
champion, Tom
Curren (left).

American, Ritchie Collins. The next day, when the final was held, the surf had dropped in size. By then Tom was really in his stride. Time and time again, Ritchie found himself taking the smaller, lower scoring waves. Although he was working the white water well, rebounding off it with some big cutbacks to the **soup**, Tom was performing with a flair that Ritchie found impossible to match. Tom outscored Collins to regain his standing in the sport. After an absence of a year, Curren was back!

Wave Sailing

The great thing about wave sailing is that it lets you sail — rather than paddle — to the place where the waves break. Wave sailing is the closest of the windsurfing disciplines to surfing. Wave boards are similar in shape to modern surfboards, but are usually a yard longer. Unlike longer windsurfing boards, they have no **daggerboard.** Because they lack volume, they tend to sink unless they are moving. This makes them difficult to get going. Wave sailors usually water start their boards by treading water next to the board and holding the sail up and out of the water. When the wind catches the sail, they can get their feet on the board and have the sail pull them up.

Most surfing maneuvers are possible on a wave board. Wave sailors have the advantage of being able to catch the waves hundreds of yards farther out to sea than surfers.

ABOVE

Aerial manuevers such as complete loops can be performed on a windsurfer.

This means that they can use more of the wave.

Because windsurfing allows you to use the power of the wind to move, as well as that of the waves, extra moves become possible. The wind provides a force for movement that is not available to surfers. The most exciting move windsurfers can make that surfers cannot is the jump. Jumps can be made off the back of a wave, off the critical section, off wind chop, and even off flat water. There are so many kinds of jumps that it would be impossible to list them all. Complete 360-degree loops are possible, either forward or backward off the wave.

Wave sailing competitors earn points for the jibes and tacks as well as for the wave riding.

Course Board Sailing and Slalom

Windsurfer Barrie Edgington rounds the buoy during a course racing competition in Curaçao in the Caribbean.

T he Professional Board Sailors Association (PBA) organizes a circuit of world events. At a professional level, the disciplines of course board sailing and slalom are the main ones, because they present the audience with a clear winner. In course racing, distances of several miles are covered. Sailors carefully plot the fastest course. The course follows a W shape across the wind. Wind strength, wind direction, and

ABOVE

The race to the
buoy in a slalom
competition often
decides who will
win.

tidal drift all affect the outcome of the race.

In slalom sailing, the course is much shorter, with many more buoys. Often these races are won, or lost, according to the sailor's speed on the jibe and tack marks. Strategy, as well as equipment, are important. A position upwind of another sailor is a great advantage, because it allows you to steal the wind from the person downwind of you — the wind goes into your sail instead of hers or his. This causes sailors to jostle for position at the start. When the horn sounds for the one-minute-to-go warning, it is important to be in position, ready to cross the line at full speed.

RIGHT

High tide at a speed competition drives the competitors (and their jeeps!) on to a narrow strip of sand.

Speed Sailing

One of the most recent developments in advanced windsurfing has been the arrival of the speed sailor. The quest is to go as fast as possible in the strongest winds. Julian Kendall, one of the pioneers of this sport, says, "The sensation of riding over water at 50 kph (about 31 mph) is like driving a car at more than three times the speed!"

Sotovento, in Fuerteventura (the Canary Islands), is perfect for speed sailing. There the world's great speed sailors, such as Pascal Maka of France, go to perfect their skills. A sand bar lies across the path of the offshore winds that sweep down from the desert sands every day during July. The surface of the water is particularly smooth at Sotovento, making it perfect for speed sailing. The course is 500 meters (about 547 yards) long and the times are electronically recorded.

The best speed sailors can reach speeds of over 44.5 knots (over 51 mph and 82 kph), and new records are set frequently. The fastest runs have been recorded in artificial trenches, in which the surface of the water is far smoother.

Some of the fastest overall speeds are set on the Mediterranean coast of France in an artificial trench filled with water.

Speed boards are specially designed for sailing along in a straight line. The rails, or edges, are hard and sharp and the boards are much narrower and shorter than other windsurfers. They have a single **fin** and no daggerboard. Near-gale force winds are required to lift the sailor and rig from the water at the start of a speed run. A speed sailor needs strength and stamina to control the power provided by the huge sails and high winds.

Speed sailing is one of the most exciting of the windsurfing disciplines, because it channels the power of the wind directly into speed. But in the end, you decide which of the three you enjoy most: course sailing, wave sailing, or speed sailing.

RIGHT

Jenna de Rosnay, now retired, one of the world's first speed sailors.

Glossary

Batten   A long, flat piece of stiff material placed into pockets of the sail to give it shape.

Bodyboard   A board made of foam used by beginners. They are usually a yard in length and are ridden lying down.

Bodysurfing   Surfing by holding your body rigid, without using any other equipment. Body surfing is only really possible in big waves.

Buoyant   Able to float. This word relates to the volume of the board. Those with high volume are more buoyant — float better — than those with low volume.

Close out   A wave that breaks along its entire length at the same time, leaving no way out for the surfer.

Critical section   The breaking section of the wave. See the photo on page 38.

Daggerboard   A type of centerboard, or fin, that helps keep windsurfers from sailing sideways. Positioned on the bottom of the board near the center, it is used along with a fin at the back of the board.

Ding   A damaged area in the board that will allow water to soak into the inner material unless mended.

Downhaul   A rope that connects the bottom corner of the sail to the bottom of the mast.

Duck dive   A technique in which the nose of the board is plunged under the wave at the last possible moment to get through white water.

Fiberglass   A hard material made of fine glass fibers woven together. It is mixed with plastic to make surfboards and windsurfers.

Fin   A protrusion, similar in shape to the dorsal fin of a dolphin, on the bottom of the board. Most surfboards have three fins near the tail. Also called skegs, they control the board in the water and act as a pivot point for turning.

Flippers   Wide, webbed footwear to help you move through the water quickly with a minimum of effort. Similar in shape to ducks' feet.

Floater   A maneuver performed on the breaking section of a wave. The surfer launches the board onto and over the breaking section, floating it down with the curl to gain speed.

Freestyle   A form of surfing or windsurfing that uses lots of tricks and maneuvers.

Gear   Windsurfing and surfing equipment.

Jibe   To turn downwind, or away from the wind.

Knot   A measurement of speed across water, about equal to 1.15 mph or 1.85 kph.

Leash   A stretchable line that attaches board to surfer. Worn around the wrist (for a bodyboard) or the ankle (for a surfboard and windsurfer).

Malibu surfing   Surfing standing up on long boards.

Neoprene   A cellular rubber material used to make wetsuits. It has good insulating properties.

Outhaul   A rope that connects the outside corner of the sail to the boom at the point farthest from the mast.

Peel   The way in which a good surfing wave breaks along its length.

Re-entry   A move in which you jump off the wave and then back on to it.

Rig   The boom, mast, and sail of a windsurfer.

Slalom   A windsurfing race with a high-wind, zig-zag course set across the wind with markers for turning.

Soup   White water after the wave has broken.

Swell   Unbroken waves. They are capable of traveling thousands of miles across the ocean without losing their energy.

Tack   To turn upwind, or toward the wind.

Tide   The rise and fall of the ocean twice a day, caused by the gravity of Sun and Moon.

Tube   A hollow tunnel formed by the curl of the wave.

Uphaul   Hoisting the sail out of the sea while standing on a windsurfer. Also the piece of rope used to perform this action.

Volume   The amount of space a board takes up. The higher its volume, the more weight it can support.

More Information

Association of Surfing Professionals (ASP)
P.O. Box 309
Huntington Beach, California 92648 USA

International Windsurfer Class Association
2006 Gladwick Street
Compton, California 90220 USA

National Scholastic Surfing Association
P.O. Box 495
Huntington Beach, California 92648 USA

United States Boardsailing Association
P.O. Box 209
Newport, Rhode Island 02840 USA

United States Surfing Federation (USSF)
11 Adams Point Road
Barrington, Rhode Island 02802 USA

Books

Fox, Frank. *Windsurfing.* Berkley, California: Amberco Press, 1987.

Hall, Major. *Sports Illustrated Boardsailing.* New York, New York: Harper and Row, 1985.

Jones, Roger. *Windsurfing: Basic and Funboard Techniques.* San Francisco, California: Harper and Row, 1985.

Lueras, Leonard. *Surfing: The Ultimate Pleasure.* New York, New York, Workman Publishing, 1984.

Wand-Tetley, Charles; and John Heath. *Boardsailing: A Beginner's Manual.* Camden, Maine: International Marine Publishing, 1986.

Young Nat. *Surfing Fundamentals.* Los Angeles, California: The Body Press, 1985.

Videos

Beginning Board Sailing Techniques.
Newport Beach, California: Alpha Video
Services, 1989.
Force 10: Sail the Gorge. Seattle
Washington: Eagle Productions, 1988.

Jibe. Reno, Nevada: Maui Magic
Instructional Videos, 1986.
Introduction to Windsurfing. Reno, Nevada:
Maui Magic Instructional Videos,
1987.

Index